An Elephant Never Forgets Its Snorkel

How Animals Survive Without Tools and Gadgets

by LISA GOLLIN EVANS

illustrated by DIANE DE GROAT

CROWN PUBLISHERS, INC. • *New York*

To Sarah and Grace
—L.G.E.

Special thanks to Frank Evans for naming this book and for his patient and helpful consultation on the text.

Text copyright © 1992 by Lisa Gollin Evans
Illustrations copyright © 1992 by Diane de Groat

Published by Crown Publishers, Inc., a Random House company, 225 Park Avenue South, New York, New York 10003

CROWN is a trademark of Crown Publishers, Inc.
Manufactured in Singapore

Library of Congress Cataloging-in-Publication Data
Evans, Lisa Gollin, 1956–
    An elephant never forgets its snorkel : how animals survive without tools and gadgets / by Lisa Gollin Evans : illustrated by Diane de Groat.
        p.   cm.
    Summary: Contains eighteen analogies between human and animal behavior, showing how animals use their bodies in place of the tools, gadgets, and equipment on which humans depend.
        1. Adaptation (Biology)—Juvenile literature. [1. Adaptation (Biology)
    2. Animals—Habits and behavior.]   I. De Groat, Diane, ill.   II. Title.
    QP82.E9   1992
    591.5—dc20   91-31828

ISBN 0-517-58401-8 (trade)
        0-517-58404-2 (lib. bdg.)

10 9 8 7 6 5 4 3 2 1   First Edition

Introduction

People have invented many things to make life easier. We use tools to build, weapons to hunt, and protective clothing and shelters to keep us comfortable. Every day we use hundreds of things that are manufactured by other people. We depend on all these things to survive.

But what if we had nothing but the bodies with which we were born? Most animals must depend upon what nature has given them. With no gadgets or equipment, they must use their bodies in unusual ways to hunt, build shelters, care for their young, and stay healthy and comfortable.

With the help of specially adapted eyes, tongues, tails, jaws, and even noses, the animals in this book accomplish amazing things without the help of tools. They can see underwater, drink through "straws," keep dry in the rain, move heavy objects, and even "snorkel"! Reading about them, you'll find out about the "animal way" of surviving in the world.

The Human Way Using a snorkel to breathe underwater.

The Animal Way When elephants swim, their giant bodies are almost totally submerged, and often only their long trunks remain above the surface of the water. Elephants "snorkel" this way, breathing through their trunks. They are surprisingly good swimmers and have been known to swim for six hours without stopping. Young elephants, called "calves," must learn to swim at an early age in order to follow their mothers through swamps and across rivers and lakes in their constant search for food. But elephants love the water and will bathe even when they are not traveling. It cools them and keeps their skin in good condition.

The snorkels that people use are puny compared to an elephant's trunk. Imagine using a snorkel that is six feet long and weighs 300 pounds!

The Human Way Wearing a rain slicker to stay dry.

The Animal Way A duck's feathers are as waterproof as a rain slicker. Ducks keep their feathers that way by constantly coating them with a layer of oil. The oil is made in glands located just above the tail. Ducks peck at this gland, then use their bills to spread the oil over their feathers. In addition to this waterproof "overcoat," ducks have an under-layer of soft, fine down feathers that keeps them warm—like a down coat. The oil-coated outer feathers protect the inner coat of down. With its insulated, waterproof coat, the duck seldom gets cold, and water almost never touches its skin!

outer feather

down feather

waterproofing the feathers

The Human Way Constructing high-rise buildings in which to live and work.

The Animal Way Tiny termites build tall mounds on the vast savannas, or grasslands, of southern Africa. The termites make a sticky "cement" out of soil, sand, and their own saliva. In the hot African sun, this cement bakes as hard as fired clay. Inside the mounds, the termites construct rooms in which they store food, lay eggs, and care for their young. They even create an air-conditioning system by building a network of ventilation ducts that carry fresh air into the mound. The termite "high-rises" can reach a height of 20 feet. That's like human beings constructing a 250-story building! There are three castes, or types, of termite: monarchs (kings and queens), soldiers, and workers. It is the role of the worker termites, always females, to build these impressive high-rises.

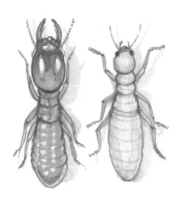

soldier   worker

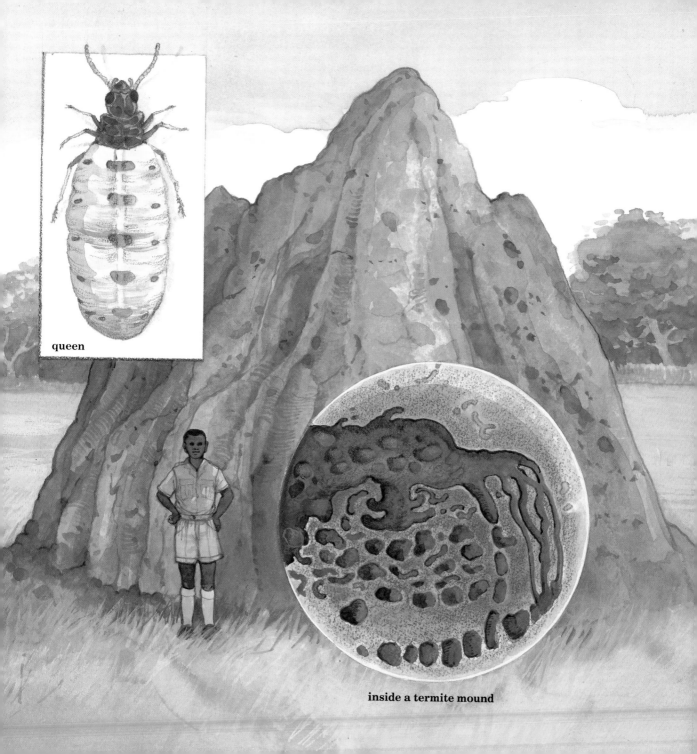

queen

inside a termite mound

The Human Way Using sunglasses to protect our eyes.

The Animal Way The polar bear tolerates the bright reflection of the sun off snow, ice, and water by closing the pupil of its eye to a hole no bigger than a pinhole. Because of this, only a very small amount of light enters the eye, and polar bears never suffer "snow blindness," as humans sometimes do. In a similar way, Eskimos made the first Arctic "sunglasses" by cutting tiny slits in pieces of bone and placing them over their eyes.

Even though polar bears can see well, they rely mainly on their remarkable sense of smell to hunt. An adult male polar bear can reach a weight of 1,600 pounds and must catch and eat one seal a week in order to survive. The seals are often hidden behind chunks of ice or in snow caves, but the polar bear's nose is so sensitive that it can smell a seal from several miles away. Polar bears are good walkers and strong swimmers and can travel many miles across the Arctic ice in search of food.

The Human Way Using bags to carry home the groceries.

The Animal Way A chipmunk's loose and floppy cheek skin creates a handy pouch for carrying food. Chipmunks gnaw the sharp edges off nuts and seeds and carefully pack their cheeks to bulging. Then they transport their booty to safe storage spaces in their underground burrows. In the fall, chipmunks are especially busy collecting food for the winter. During the winter, they sleep on top of their store of food so they do not have to leave the safety and warmth of their burrows to look for more. As winter wears on, the chipmunks sink lower and lower into their edible beds.

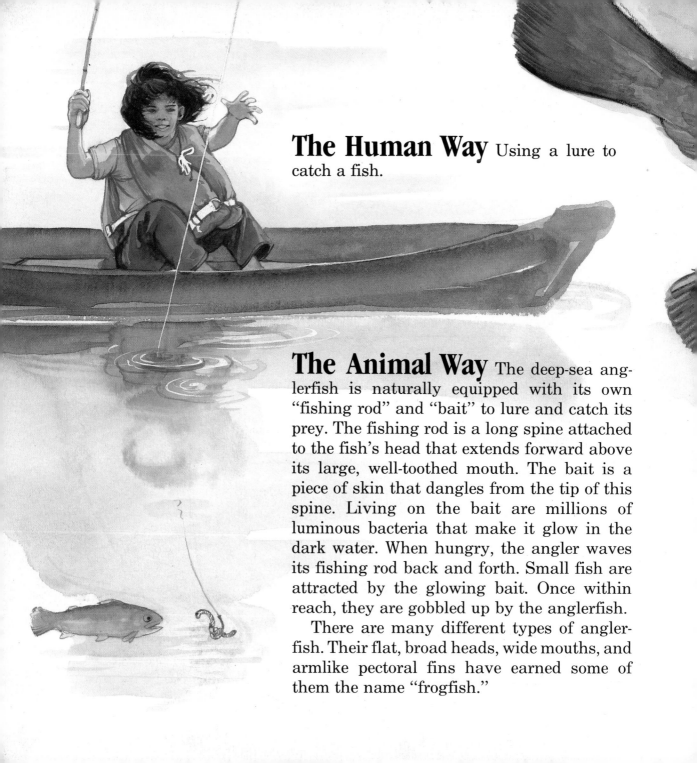

The Human Way Using a lure to catch a fish.

The Animal Way The deep-sea anglerfish is naturally equipped with its own "fishing rod" and "bait" to lure and catch its prey. The fishing rod is a long spine attached to the fish's head that extends forward above its large, well-toothed mouth. The bait is a piece of skin that dangles from the tip of this spine. Living on the bait are millions of luminous bacteria that make it glow in the dark water. When hungry, the angler waves its fishing rod back and forth. Small fish are attracted by the glowing bait. Once within reach, they are gobbled up by the anglerfish.

There are many different types of anglerfish. Their flat, broad heads, wide mouths, and armlike pectoral fins have earned some of them the name "frogfish."

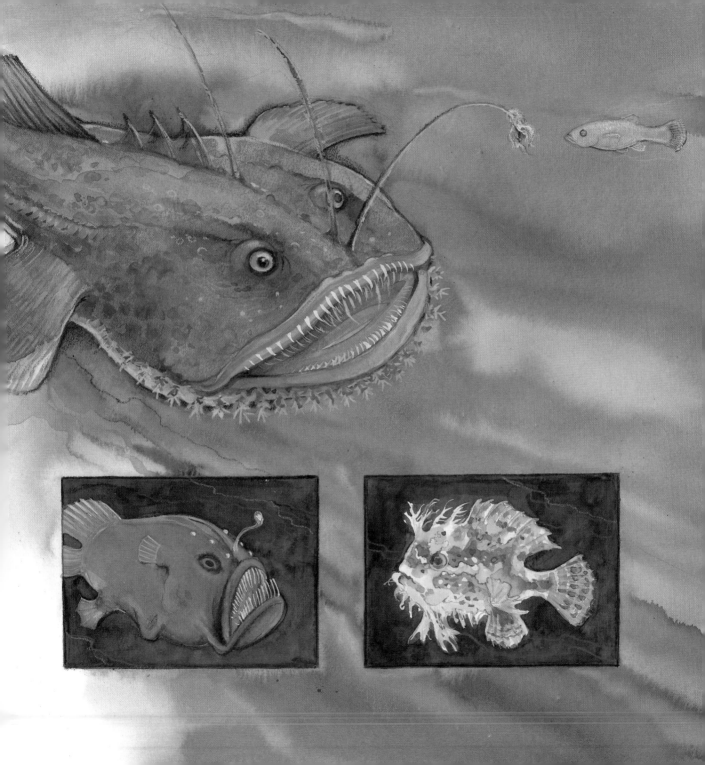

The Human Way Using a straw to drink from a bottle.

The Animal Way Hummingbirds use their long beaks and tongues to reach deep into flowers and feed on nectar hidden there. Nectar is a sugary liquid that is made by the plant. Once the hummingbird's beak is inside the flower, it extends its long, slim white tongue. The end of the tongue is divided into two parts, each of which curls inward to make a tube. By licking the inside of the flower, the humming-bird collects the nectar, then draws it through its tongue into its mouth. A hummingbird's lick is very fast—about 13 licks a second. Although they are small, hummingbirds are very active, fast-moving birds, and for this reason they need a lot of food. A hummingbird may visit as many as 1,000 blossoms in a day and eat half its weight in sugar. That's the equivalent of a ten-year-old child eating 320 candy bars a day!

hummingbird tongue

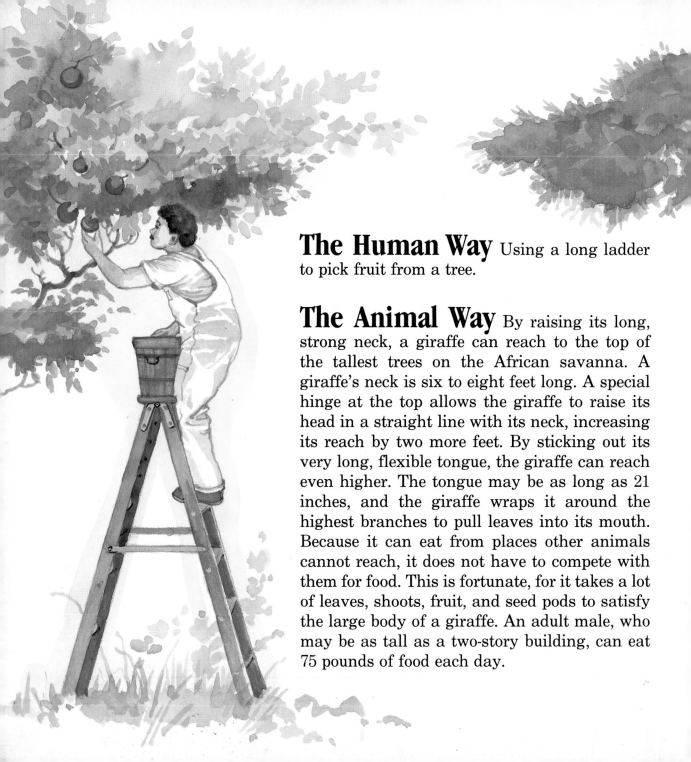

The Human Way Using a long ladder to pick fruit from a tree.

The Animal Way By raising its long, strong neck, a giraffe can reach to the top of the tallest trees on the African savanna. A giraffe's neck is six to eight feet long. A special hinge at the top allows the giraffe to raise its head in a straight line with its neck, increasing its reach by two more feet. By sticking out its very long, flexible tongue, the giraffe can reach even higher. The tongue may be as long as 21 inches, and the giraffe wraps it around the highest branches to pull leaves into its mouth. Because it can eat from places other animals cannot reach, it does not have to compete with them for food. This is fortunate, for it takes a lot of leaves, shoots, fruit, and seed pods to satisfy the large body of a giraffe. An adult male, who may be as tall as a two-story building, can eat 75 pounds of food each day.

The Human Way Using snowshoes to travel in the snow.

The Animal Way The long, broad hind feet of the snowshoe hare stop it from sinking into deep snow. Like snowshoes, the big feet spread the hare's weight over a large area, allowing it to walk or run where animals with smaller feet would sink. The hare also grows long fur on the sides of its feet and between its toes to keep its feet warm and prevent them from slipping on frozen snow and ice.

"Snowshoes" are also worn by the white-tailed ptarmigan, an unusual bird that lives in the Arctic and in mountainous areas of Canada and the western United States. The ptarmigan has wide-toed feet that are covered with white feathers in the winter—even between its toes and up the full length of its legs. Like the broad feet of the snowshoe hare, the ptarmigan's feathered toes prevent it from sinking into soft snow.

ptarmigan foot

The Human Way Using a fly swatter to swat a fly.

The Animal Way An elephant's tail is an excellent fly swatter. Bare except for long, thick, wiry hairs at its end, it is perfect for swatting flies and other insects off the animal's back and legs. It would not make a good fly swatter for people, however: an average elephant tail weighs more than 20 pounds, and each of its hairs is as thick as a piece of spaghetti!

This type of tail is also found on giraffes and rhinoceros. Besides having a built-in fly swatter, elephants and rhinos get help from birds called "oxpeckers," who ride on their backs. These birds eat the insects that gather around the large animals.

elephant tail

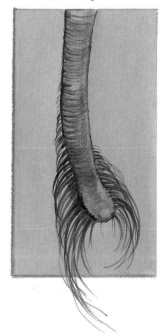

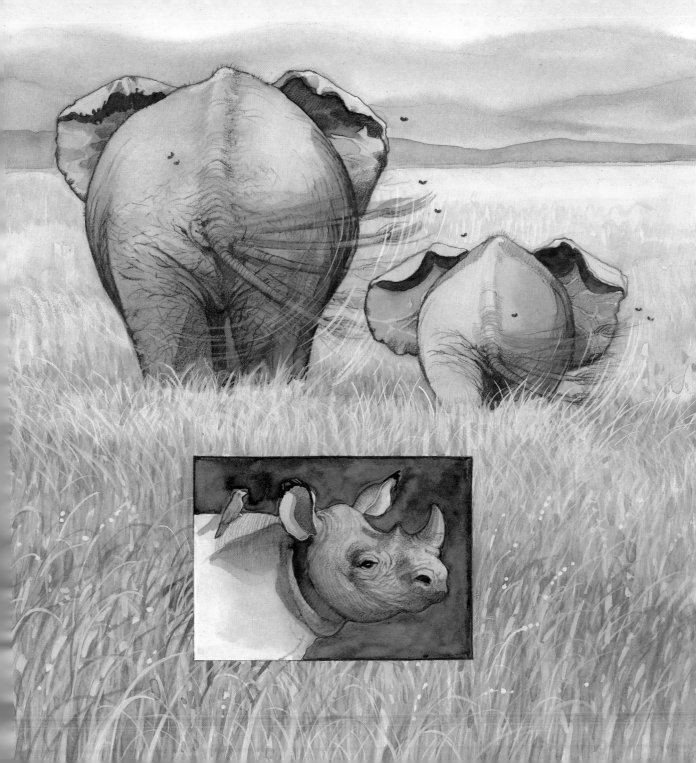

The Human Way Keeping cows on a dairy farm.

The Animal Way Some types of ants keep "ant cows" in their colonies. These ant cows are tiny pear-shaped insects called "aphids." During the day, the ants herd the aphids to a plant, where they feed by sucking a sugary liquid called "honeydew" from the stems. At night, the ants drive the aphids off the plant to an underground chamber or other sheltered spot where they are safe from predators. The ants keep the "cows" for their honeydew and "milk" them by stroking the aphids' bodies with their antennae. This causes the aphids to release drops of honeydew, which are quickly gobbled up by the ants. When winter arrives, the ants take their aphids and aphid eggs to their nests, where they take care of them until spring. In spring, the ants herd the newly hatched aphids to plants for grazing.

The Human Way Using goggles, a noseclip, earplugs, and fins while swimming.

The Animal Way Beavers are fully equipped for living and working in the water. They have transparent inner eyelids that act like goggles, protecting their eyes while allowing them to see underwater. Their ears and nostrils have valves that close to keep the water out, and their hind feet are webbed, making them powerful swimmers. Other things that help beavers live in the water include waterproof fur, furry lips that seal behind their large "buckteeth" to keep the water out of their mouths, and a large flat tail that acts like a rudder when they swim. Young beavers, called "kits," quickly learn to be at home in the water. Kits are able to swim within a half hour of their birth.

hind foot

The Human Way Using camouflage clothes to hide in the woods.

The Animal Way The extremely slow two-toed sloth of South America spends most of its life hanging upside down from tree branches, where it benefits from a very unusual method of camouflage. The sloth's long-haired coat provides a home for microscopic green plants called "algae." The algae grow in grooves on the sloth's hair and turn the sloth a greenish color. In the dim light of the forest, the sloth blends in with the surrounding leaves. Consequently, jaguars and eagles, the sloth's chief enemies, have a tough time finding them. Like a bird watcher in the woods, the sloth also stays hidden by keeping still. To move the distance of one foot along a branch takes the sloth about half an hour.

The Human Way Using an umbrella as shelter from the rain.

The Animal Way In the rain, squirrels can be seen curling their long, full tails over their heads to keep themselves dry. When the weather gets cold, and while hibernating during winter, squirrels also use their furry tails as "blankets," wrapping them around their bodies to keep warm. In hot countries, squirrels have found other uses for their tails. Ground squirrels in the Kalahari Desert of Africa keep cool by using their tails as parasols, angling them over their heads to shade themselves from the hot sun.

The Human Way Using a forklift to move a heavy load.

The Animal Way Among some species of harvester ants there are large-headed worker ants with very strong jaws. These workers can lift more than 50 times their own weight in their jaws—the equivalent of a man lifting nearly four tons, the weight of a small elephant! Harvester ants are common in the western United States, where they build large mound-shaped anthills. Inside the anthill are many chambers and tunnels in which the ants raise their young, store seeds, and spend the winter. The workers serve the queen ant, who is the mother of every ant in the colony. Workers do the jobs that keep the colony healthy and thriving, including caring for the ant larvae until they hatch, gathering seeds for food, and feeding and bathing the queen ant.

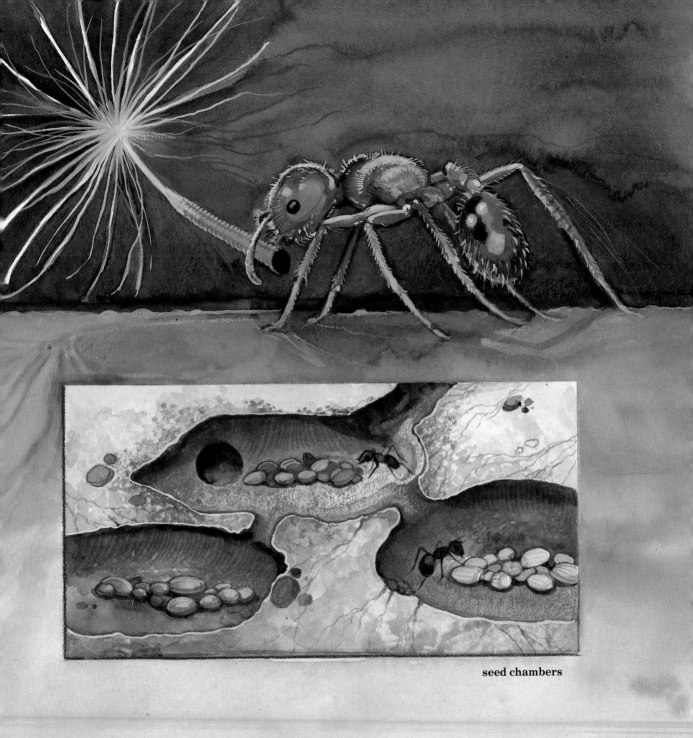

seed chambers

The Human Way Using a carrier for transporting a baby.

The Animal Way Kangaroos are "marsupials"—mammals that carry their young in special pouches. When kangaroos are born, they are only the size of lima beans. The tiny babies, called "joeys," wriggle from birth openings into their mothers' pouches and nurse from nipples inside. The joeys use the pouch until they are about ten months old and too big to remain there. During this time, they sleep in the pouch and hide in it when enemies come near. Like a baby in a carrier, the joey looks at the world from a snug and safe place. Because she has a pouch, a kangaroo mother does not need to leave her young while she searches for food.

Koalas also are marsupials and carry their babies in pouches until they are about eight months old. Then the young koalas climb onto their mothers' backs, where they cling until they are about one year of age.

joey

The Human Way Using a flashlight to see in the dark.

The Animal Way The unusual flashlight fish has oval-shaped "lights" on its head that are bright enough to cast beams of light several inches through the dark water. The light is made by billions of luminous bacteria that live in pouchlike organs below the fish's eyes. The fish uses its "flashlights" to search for worms and other small water creatures that it eats. But the light also attracts predators that hunt the flashlight fish. When predators approach, the flashlight fish can escape being seen by raising a fold of black skin over its glowing pouches, like an upside-down eyelid. Other animals make light for communication or for attracting food, but flashlight fish are believed to be the only animals that use their light to look for food. The flashlight fish lives off the coast of Madagascar and Indonesia and in the Red Sea.

The Human Way Driving motor homes from place to place.

The Animal Way A turtle carries its "home" wherever it goes. Its hard shell provides safety from its enemies and shelter from the weather. When a turtle believes that it is in danger, it pulls its legs, head, and neck into its shell. Some shells even have hinged openings that can be closed after the turtle's head and legs are pulled inside. But unlike people, turtles cannot leave their homes, because their shells are part of their skeletons. The turtle's ribs and backbone are attached to the bony plates that make up the shell. But not all turtle shells provide safe retreats. Sea turtles, for example, have only small shells relative to their size, and although the shells provide protection for the turtle's body, there is no room for its head and legs.

turtle skeleton

Lisa Gollin Evans is a graduate of Cornell University and the University of California at Berkeley and is a member of the state bar of Massachusetts. She lives in Marblehead, Massachusetts, and is the author of a book for parents, *Hiking with Children in Rocky Mountain National Park*. This is her first book for children.

Diane de Groat studied fine art at the Pratt Institute in Brooklyn, New York. She has since illustrated many books for children, including *Animal Fact/Animal Fable* and *Little Rabbit's Loose Tooth* for Crown. She lives in Chappaqua, New York.